Trekking in Nepal

Written by Janine Scott

Photography by Don Higgins, Amanda Thomas, and Peter Sahrmann

Nepal

Zoe travels from her home in New Zealand to trek in Nepal. From the moment she arrives in Kathmandu, she is fascinated by the lives of the people she encounters. The lives they lead are so different from her own in a modern city in the Pacific. She soon learns to respect their very different ways but also finds that she has many things in common with the people of Nepal.

respect to place a high value on something

Contents

Trekking in Nepal

My name is Zoe. My dad has a great job. He travels
around the world, taking photographs of fascinating
people in fascinating places. For the first time,
Dad is taking our family with him. We are going
to Nepal to trek in the Annapurna foothills. At last,
we will have the chance to see with our very own eyes
all that Dad photographs!

Annapurna
(26,504 feet)

Pokhara

Kathmandu

NEPAL

foothill   a hill at the base of a mountain

Day 1

We arrived in Kathmandu, the capital of Nepal. The smells, noises, and people were all exciting. There were motorbikes everywhere. People were buying dumplings at roadside stalls. There were monkeys outside the temples and monks and holy men walking in the streets. After three days of sightseeing, my family was exhausted. We were ready to leave the busy city and start our peaceful trek in the foothills.

Day 4

The bus trip to Pokhara, Nepal's second largest city, was an eight-hour drive—not very restful after all! It was very, very hot, but we found the countryside fascinating. I watched the people working in their rice fields. I liked it when the bus stopped. All the children rushed up to us. They always smiled and laughed. Some of them had never seen a digital camera before. They loved seeing instant pictures of themselves. Mind you, I had never seen a buffalo up close before!

Day 5

We started our trek today. Our guide was friendly. The uphill walk through the flowering rhododendron forests was not too tiring. It was interesting to see plants that we have in our garden back home growing in their wild state. There was plenty of time for Dad to take photographs and for us to rest. At one village, the children greeted us with, "Namaste!" This means "I bow to you." By the end of the first day, my legs were happy to arrive at the camp.

rhododendron   an evergreen tree with large leaves and bright flowers

Day 6

This was a day to remember. There were leeches
everywhere! Our guide made us put salt on our socks
and boots to keep the leeches away. He also carried
thin cotton bags with salt inside them. He pressed
a bag against any leeches that got on us.

The mountains were breathtaking, but I forgot to look
at the scenery most of the day. I did not even have time
to be scared on the bridges. I was too busy looking out
for leeches. They like the wet jungle—and our blood!
We had a contest to see who got the most bites. I was
so glad I did not win.

Are there animals
in your country
that can harm you?

breathtaking   astonishing

Some local people invited us into their home in the evening. It was dark inside the house, but it had a very warm, welcoming feeling. Later on, things were not so warm. The monsoon rains came, and a river of rain ran through our tent.

Learn About Leeches

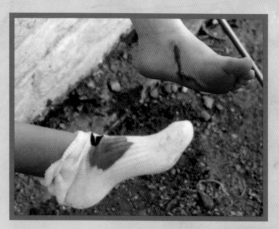

A leech is a worm with a sucker at each end of its body. Some leeches are parasitic, feeding on the blood of animals or people. Other leeches live on dead or decaying plants and animals. Leeches make a wound in the skin to suck out the blood. They also produce a chemical liquid that thins the blood. This causes a leech bite to bleed for a long time.

Long ago, doctors used leeches to treat many illnesses. They thought that these animals sucked out the patient's bad blood. Today, doctors have started to use leeches again. Leeches suck excess blood from wounds after operations in which fingers and hands have been reattached to a person.

In the afternoon, we swam in Chicken River and lay in the sun on the warm, flat rocks. It was wonderful to take a rest from walking.

It was all downhill this morning. This part of the trip was much easier. We were making our way back down to the valley floor.

This night was fun. The locals entertained us with traditional Nepalese music and dance. We all joined in. They laughed at our dancing.

Day 9

It was hot today, and we were hiking uphill. It was hard
work. We walked beside green rice fields before we went
up, up, up. I struggled for part of the day. Night had its
surprises, too. Hailstones the size of marbles hit our tent,
but I was so tired that even the flashes of lightning and
loud thunder didn't keep me awake for long. I needed
my rest for the final hike out of the foothills tomorrow.

Day 13

A few days have passed. The leeches, the lightning, and the long uphill climbs now seem like a distant memory. Two highlights of my Nepal trip were going downriver in a canoe and riding on an elephant. We even washed the elephant in the river. It washed us, too, by giving us all a shower with its trunk. Luckily, we had changed into our swimsuits. I was glad Dad took photographs of our trip. I can't wait to show them to my class back in New Zealand!

Explore Nepal

Nepal is nestled between India in the south and Tibet and China in the north. Today, there are many different groups of people living in Nepal. In the past, most people came from India and Tibet.

In northern Nepal, there are steep mountains covered with snow. The highest mountain in the world, Mt. Everest, is found there. To the south lies a flat, fertile river plain that has been made into farmland. This area used to be covered with thick jungle.

fertile   producing large, healthy crops

Nepal's capital and largest city is Kathmandu. It is famous for its many temples.

On the Go!

What are the Sherpa people also called?
Go to page 16

What are prayer stones, prayer wheels, and prayer flags used for in Nepal?
Go to page 19

What mysterious creature is supposed to live in Nepal?
Go to page 22

CHINA

NEPAL

TIBET

Mt. Everest

Kathmandu

INDIA

Tigers of the Snow

When people hear the word "Sherpa," they usually think of mountain guides. However, the word "Sherpa" refers to a group of people living in the Himalayan mountains in northeast Nepal. The Sherpa people originally came from Tibet. They have been nicknamed "tigers of the snow," as they are strong and agile. They live at high altitudes in cold, rugged areas.

The steep mountains in Nepal often make it impossible to build roads. Instead, people use animals, such as yaks, to transport items from place to place. These animals can live at high altitudes. Mules also carry heavy loads, and people carry goods on their backs, too. Since the 1950s, Sherpa porters have been hired to carry heavy loads up and down the mountains for tourists and people on climbing treks.

agile   able to move quickly and easily

There is less oxygen in the air the higher you go up a mountain. People who live at high altitudes have large lungs and thick, red blood cells to help them breathe more easily.

A Famous Sherpa

Many Sherpa people use the word "Sherpa" as their surname, because it is a highly respected name, made famous by Sherpa Tenzing Norgay (above). Tenzing Norgay and Sir Edmund Hillary, of New Zealand, were the first two people to successfully climb to the top of Mt. Everest. However, there is more than one Sherpa surname. There are 18 clan surnames in all.

Tourists and Treks

Tourists play an important part in the daily life of Nepal. People come from all over the world to climb Mt. Everest, trek in the Himalayan foothills, and sightsee in Kathmandu. However, tourists can have a major impact on the environment, so people now pay fees if they enter national parks and conservation areas. These fees are put toward projects that help educate people, develop conservation programs, and preserve the surroundings. Mountaineers must take their trash with them when they leave.

How does tourism help your country? Does it harm it in any way?

Donations from organizations such as the Himalayan Trust help build airfields in Nepal. The Himalayan Trust was founded by Sir Edmund Hillary.

Bringing Good Luck

Prayer stones with symbols carved or painted on them can be found throughout Nepal. Often the stones are there to ask for protection for people who are traveling in dangerous mountain areas.

Prayer wheels are also found all over Nepal. People, including tourists going on treks, spin these around in the hope of being blessed with good fortune. Prayer flags are a common sight, too. People believe that the winds will carry their prayers to heaven.

Teahouse, Schoolhouse

Many local people run teahouses. These are guest houses for tourists. In Nepal, travelers from overseas can go on teahouse treks. They trek during the day and then stay at teahouses every night, rather than in tents. There they can share stories, a hot meal, and a pot of spicy, milky tea.

Since the 1960s, more than 25 schools have been set up in Nepal. Some of these schools were started to educate Sherpa children in the Mt. Everest region. More recently, the Himalayan Trust has set up training programs for Nepalese teachers. Teachers from around the world come to Nepal to train others to be teachers.

A cup of tea in Nepal can be sweet, salty, or spicy. Black pepper or ginger may even go into the pot!

Donations help buy desks, chairs, and learning materials, such as paper, pencils, and books. Some schools build libraries, too.

21

Yetis and Yaks

Nepal is famous for the yeti. The Sherpa people gave this name to a white, hairy, apelike creature, which is also known as the Abominable Snowman. This creature is believed to live on Mt. Everest and in the Himalaya region. Some people claim they have sighted the creature, and some have found large footprints in the snow. There have even been expeditions to search for the yeti. However, no evidence has ever been found to prove that it really exists.

Another famous hairy creature from Nepal is the yak. These animals are found in the mountains, as high as 16,000 feet above sea level. Their long, shaggy hair keeps them warm.

What other countries have mythical creatures? Do you believe in them?

Some mountain people are yak herders. They raise yaks for their wool and milk.

23

What Do You Think?

1   Why is it important for people to visit other countries around the world?

How does traveling to another country teach you to respect different ways of life?

2   If you had traveled to Nepal with Zoe, what would you have found different about the traditions?

Index